Women's Guide to Demystifying E-commerce

Joyce Audrey Ford

Table of Contents

In the modern world of business, it is useless to be a creative, original thinker unless you can also sell what you create. Management cannot be expected to recognize a good idea unless it is presented to them by a good salesman.

— David Ogilvy

Chapter 1. Introduction

Special Report: A Women's Guide to Demystifying E-commerce

Are you a woman seeking to navigate the bustling lanes of e-commerce? If so, this special report just might be your compass! Gingerly crafted to suit both novices and seasoned e-commerce enthusiasts alike, our report takes you by the hand, bringing clarity to the usually intimidating technical jargon. We unravel the complex world of digital shopping carts, online payments, and customer engagement, turning them into relatable, plain English. This Special Report, "A Woman's Guide to Demystifying E-commerce," is the buoyant, engaging, and comprehensive guide you've been waiting for. It is sure to leave you feeling confident, informed, and ready to master the e-commerce universe! Don't let technicalities eclipse your potential - seize this user-friendly guide today and pave your path to e-commerce proficiency!

Chapter 2. Understanding the E-commerce Landscape

In today's business climate, e-commerce stands as the epitome of economic evolution - a bustling digital bazaar that binds businesses and customers across continents. If you find yourself daunted by the jargons or the sheer scale of it, fear not! Our first step in unraveling the enigma of e-commerce starts with understanding its sprawling landscape.

2.1. What is E-commerce?

In simple terms, e-commerce refers to electronic commerce. It's the art and science of buying and selling products and services over the internet. E-commerce may encompass a vast array of transactions, from traditional retail business to auction or music sites, from delivering services digitally like software or e-learning to trading various types of products, both tangible and intangible.

2.2. Categories of E-commerce

Primarily, e-commerce can be categorized into four types depending on the entities involved in the transaction.

- Business to Consumer (B2C): Here, businesses sell to consumers. Think of your typical online retail portals like Amazon and eBay where you go to purchase a product from a business.

- Business to Business (B2B): In B2B model, one business sells a product or service to another business. A typical example could be a software developed by a business targeted at other organizations.

- Consumer to Business (C2B): This is a flipped version of standard business frameworks where the consumer provides services or products to businesses. An example would be a freelance designer creating logos for companies.

- Consumer to Consumer (C2C): In this model, consumers are both the buyers and sellers interacting in an online marketplace. Platforms like eBay and Etsy allow individuals to sell their products to other consumers.

Understanding these categories can assist in aligning your business requirements with the right e-commerce model.

2.3. Benefits of E-commerce

The flourishing scale of e-commerce is an outcome of the multifold benefits it brings along.

- Global Reach: E-commerce vaporizes geographical boundaries and time restrictions. Your online store is open 24/7 to a worldwide audience.

- Lower Costs: The digital nature of business can save costs involved with a physical location, staffing and so on. These savings can then translate into lower prices or higher margins.

- Convenience: Customers can browse, compare, and purchase goods from the comfort of their homes.

- Wider Range of Products: Customers aren't limited by shelf space and can hence explore a broader array of products.

- Personalization: Based on customer preferences, businesses can offer personalized deals, recommendations, and shopping experiences.

2.4. Common Challenges in E-commerce

While the e-commerce landscape offers an ocean of opportunities, it is not without certain challenges.

- Internet Accessibility: E-commerce is heavily reliant on internet access. Regions with spotty internet availability can pose significant barriers.

- Security Concerns: Maintaining the security of digital transactions and data privacy can be a constant concern.

- Delivery and Logistics: Delivering products to international locations with different customs and regulations can be tricky.

- Online Trust: Building customer trust without physical interaction or experience of the product can be challenging.

- Technology Adoption: Both the business and the consumers need to adapt to the technology to make e-commerce transactions successful.

2.5. Keys to a Successful E-commerce Business

A successful e-commerce venture is not a matter of chance. It is the outcome of careful planning and the execution of a clear and comprehensive strategy. Few key aspects include:

- Providing High-Quality Products/Services: The cornerstone of any successful business, ensuring a high-quality product or service creates repeat customers and brand advocates.

- User-Friendly Website Design: Navigability, aesthetic appeal, and functional design can significantly impact the customers' buying decision.

- Effective Digital Marketing: Utilizing digital channels effectively can drive traffic, improve conversions, and enhance brand visibility.

- Stellar Customer Service: Excellent customer service fosters customer trust and retention.

- Data Security: Implementing robust security measures to protect customer data boosts customer confidence.

In conclusion, understanding the e-commerce landscape requires not just familiarity with the technicalities but also an appreciation for its myriad possibilities and potential challenges. With a firm grasp on what e-commerce encompasses, your journey into the world of digital commerce is off to a great start. With each subsequent chapter, we will delve deeper into the particulars of setting up and growing your e-commerce business.

Chapter 3. E-commerce Platforms: Choosing the Right Fit

Beginning the voyage into the e-commerce world, one of the first choices you must deliberate over is selecting an appropriate e-commerce platform to establish your online store. The platform acts as the digital foundation for your business, making the choice an essential piece of your e-commerce puzzle. This chapter aims to demystify this crucial process for you, elaborating on the core features to consider, the types of platforms available, their pros and cons, and tips to ensure a seamless selection process.

3.1. Understanding E-commerce Platforms

E-commerce platforms are comprehensive software applications that allow businesses to sell products and services online. These platforms handle a variety of operations, including displaying your inventory, managing online transactions, tracking orders, and even promoting customer interactions. E-commerce platforms come in all shapes and sizes, with varying degrees of complexity, customization possibilities, and pricing models. The optimal choice is contingent upon your unique needs, business goals, technical expertise, and budget.

3.2. Identifying Essential Features in an E-commerce Platform

Before embarking on your e-commerce platform selection journey, you must first identify the essential features that are non-negotiable for your online business operations. Here are some pointers:

- **Website builder**: This feature allows you to design your online store without advanced technical knowledge. It should offer a variety of templates, customizability, quick update features, and mobile-friendly designs.

- **Product management**: Look for a system that facilitates easy addition, modification, and removal of products. Essential traits include multiple product categories, stock management capabilities, and variant options for products like size or color.

- **Payment and security**: Your selected platform should support various payment methods such as credit cards, debit cards, and mobile wallets. It should also guarantee top-grade security to safeguard customer information.

- **Search Engine Optimization (SEO)**: A platform that has built-in SEO features will enhance your store's visibility on search engines, pulling more traffic, and hence sales.

- **Customer support**: Excellent customer service is crucial for troubleshooting and user assistance. Multiple support channels and quick response times are beneficial.

- **Marketing tools**: The platform should provide promotional capabilities like email marketing, social media integration, discount codes, and customer reviews.

- **Analytics**: A robust analytics system is necessary to track your store's performance, understand customer behaviors, and optimize operations.

3.3. Comparing Types of E-commerce Platforms

E-commerce platforms can generally be classified into four broad categories: open-source, self-hosted, cloud-based, and social media storefronts. Here, we compare these types, shedding light on their strengths and weaknesses.

- **Open-source platforms**: Open-source platforms, like Magento, provide unrivaled customization options since their source code is accessible and modifiable. However, they demand considerable technical expertise and could entail hidden expenses like web hosting, security certifications, and developer fees.

- **Self-hosted platforms**: These platforms offer hosting as part of their package, reducing the burden of technical maintenance. However, they often have less flexibility than open-source options. Shopify is a popular self-hosted platform.

- **Cloud-based platforms**: Cloud-based options, like BigCommerce, manage hosting and software maintenance, making them perfect for non-tech savvy individuals. However, they could lead to higher long-term costs and bounded customization.

- **Social media storefronts**: Platforms like Facebook Shops allow selling directly from your social media page, thereby leveraging your pre-existing follower base. However, they also limit customization and can become expensive with transaction fees.

3.4. Making the Right Choice

Choosing the right e-commerce platform boils down to several factors:

- **Your skill level**: If you're tech-savvy, an open-source platform might be a good fit. If not, consider cloud-based or self-hosted platforms.

- **Budget constraints**: Remember to factor in not just the upfront cost of the platform but also hosting expenses, transaction costs, add-on features, and cost of potential customization.

- **Scale of operations**: If your plan is for large-scale operations, ensure the platform can handle high traffic and product volumes.

- **Specific needs**: Have unique needs? Make sure the chosen platform can cater to them either natively or through integrations.

In conclusion, the selection of an e-commerce platform is a significant decision that necessitates careful evaluation of your business needs, financial capacity, and technical prowess. Remember, this platform will be the foundation stone of your online business, so spend ample time deliberating over your decision before making the final choice. The right platform can catalyze your online success, fostering a smooth journey in the dynamic world of e-commerce.

Chapter 4. Setting Up Your Online Store: A Step by Step Guide

In this incredibly enriching and enlightening segment, we step into the promising domain of setting up your online store. This chapter functions as a comprehensive, step-by-step guide, effectively demystifying the intricacies of the process. It is a journey into owning a digital storefront, setting up its skeletal framework, and imbuing it with a semblance of your business vision. So, gear up and brace yourself as we delve into this detailed and elaborate process, ensuring you have the requisite tools and knowledge to initiate your e-commerce expedition.

4.1. Initiation and Planning

The first essential step in setting up your online store is the initiation and planning phase. This essentially involves identifying and specifying the primary purpose, goals, and objectives of your online store. One of the critical elements includes defining your target audience. Analyzing your existing customer base and analyzing potential customers based on demographics, location, profession, preferences, and lifestyle can set the foundation for your strategic decision-making process. Moreover, create a comprehensive plan for products or services you intend to offer on your digital storefront and take considerable time in understanding your competition.

4.2. Selecting an E-commerce Platform

Once you have the basics in place, the second step involves choosing an appropriate e-commerce platform. The market is saturated with diverse options; therefore, you need to be judicious while making your selection. Take into account factors such as budget, scalability, security, search engine optimization, mobile-friendly capabilities, and easy-to-use interface. Research widely employed platforms like Shopify, WooCommerce, BigCommerce, and Magento, including their functionalities, pricing structures, and customer reviews. Make sure your chosen platform offers services that align with your business aspirations.

4.3. Designing the Website

The third step, after selecting the e-commerce platform, is designing your website. This undertaking encapsulates one of the most significant elements of customer impression and engagement. Treat your website as a digital mirror of your business's personality. Incorporate brand colors, logos, and taglines consistently across all pages. The layout should be clean, intuitive, and easy-to-navigate. Ensure that the design is mobile-responsive and includes call-to-action buttons. Remember, a well-architected site simply leads to a more enjoyable shopping experience for your customers.

4.4. Website Navigation and User Experience

The fourth step focuses on website navigation and user experience (UX), which are intrinsically linked. Display clear product categories, subcategories, and keep the search functionality at prominent spots. Use breadcrumbs for better navigation and to indicate the users' location on your site. Make sure that the checkout process is straightforward, without too many steps or necessary fields. Offer guest checkout to accommodate customers who do not wish to create an account.

4.5. Product Upload and Description

The fifth step of setting up your online store involves uploading the product details. Create a unique SKU (Stock Keeping Unit) for each item while including clear, high-resolution images. Pay significant attention to creating compelling product descriptions using an engaging tone and incorporating relevant keywords for better SEO performance. The products should be categorized accurately with appropriate tags and filters to aid customers in their search.

4.6. Secure Checkout and Payment Gateway Integration

The sixth step involves setting up a secure checkout and integrating a reliable payment gateway. The payment gateway should be versatile enough to support various payment options such as credit cards, debit cards, digital wallets, and net banking. Prioritize applying an SSL certificate to ensure a secure environment for transactions. Information privacy is paramount, so reassure customers of their data's safety and security.

4.7. Shipping and Return policies

The seventh step constitutes drafting comprehensible shipping and return policies. These should be explicit and easily accessible from the product and checkout pages. Buyers must clearly understand delivery timelines, shipping charges, and procedure in case of product returns or refunds. Thoroughly articulated policies reduce customer apprehension and help build customer trust.

4.8. Launch and Testing

Finally, after all these stages, comes the grand launch. However, this is invariably coupled with rigorous testing. Beta-testing is typically performed by a select group of users who can test the website's full functionality. Also, perform A/B testing including elements like headlines, color schemes, page layouts, images, etc to determine which version garners better user response. After all issues have been addressed and enhancements have been made, proceed with the public launch of your online store.

Each of these steps constitutes the critical milestones in your journey of setting up an online store. Success isn't achieved overnight, and it's the continuous effort of refining based on user feedback and staying updated with the latest e-commerce trends that make your online store shine among a myriad of others. Remember, patience, and persistence are the keys to navigating the multi-layered world of e-commerce.

Chapter 5. Pricing and Inventory Management: Balancing Act

E-commerce is often presented as a glamorous initiation into boundless online commerce, but behind the scenes, a series of decisions and carefully calibrated strategies are continually set in motion. Among these crucial decisions are your approach to pricing and your techniques for managing inventory No business can thrive without getting these two fundamental pieces of the puzzle right.

5.1. Setting the Right Price

Price is not merely a numerical reflection of value - it's a statement about your business, your brand, and your commitment to customers. It's a major factor influencing a buyer's decision to click 'add to cart' or move on to your competitor Unsurprisingly, getting your pricing strategy right can make the difference between surviving in the e-commerce space or fading into oblivion.

The ideal pricing strategy depends on various factors, such as the price sensitivity of your target market, your cost, the competitive landscape, and value perception. Let's take a detailed look at each of these factors:

- **Target Market Price Sensitivity**: In some markets, a price difference of a few dollars can cause consumers to switch brands, while in others, consumers willingly pay a premium for perceived value or brand reputation. To ascertain the price sensitivity of your target market, investing in solid market research is vital.

- **Cost**: The cost of your product should always be a primary guiding factor in any pricing decision. Your online store needs to cover its costs and make a profit. If the price you set cannot cover the cost of the goods, the overhead, and a fair margin, your e-commerce business will not survive for long.

- **Competition**: E-commerce is often intensely competitive, with price comparisons only a click away, and competitive pricing strategy is therefore very important. Understanding your competitors' pricing is essential in deciding where you want to position yourself in the market.

- **Value Perception**: Price is often a reflection of perceived value. If your product provides added value, whether through superior quality, innovative design, or exceptional service, you can charge a premium price. To do this, however, you need to communicate this added value effectively to your customers.

5.2. Inventory Management: The Balancing Act

Once you've settled on your pricing strategy, the next vital matter is managing your inventory. In e-commerce, inventory management is even more critical since it's all about balancing the act - holding enough stock to satisfy your customers' demands but not too much that ties up your capital and storage space.

Proper inventory management can help you avoid stockouts and overstocks. Here are some key steps to achieve this balance:

- **Demand Forecasting**: This is the practice of predicting what your customers will buy in the future using historical sales data, market trends, seasonal trends, and promotional activities. It is the cornerstone of effective inventory management.

- **Safety Stock**: Safety stock is the extra inventory you keep on hand to guard against variability in market demand or lead time. It enables you to meet unforeseen spikes in demand and helps to prevent stock-outs.

- **Reorder Point**: This is the level of inventory at which you should place a new order to replenish your stock before it runs out. Calculation of the reorder point involves factors like the lead time demand and safety stock.

- **Invest in Inventory Management Software**: Robust software helps to track stock levels, sales, and orders in real-time, providing you with valuable insights to optimize your inventory management.

5.3. Using Technological Tools

Both pricing strategy and inventory management can be significantly enhanced using modern technology tools that use artificial intelligence and machine learning algorithms. These sophisticated tools can analyze large volumes of data much more quickly and accurately than any human, providing insights and recommendations regarding optimal pricing and inventory levels. They can help you increase operational efficiency, maximize profits, and improve customer satisfaction, thereby giving you a competitive advantage in the e-commerce landscape.

Remember, the digital world of e-commerce brings both enormous opportunities and challenges. Mastering the necessary techniques of Pricing and Inventory Management is a true Balancing Act, but with careful planning, strategy, and the use of available tools, you can pave your path to success.

Chapter 6. Navigating Online Payments: Options and Security

Online transactions constitute a significant part of the e-commerce process, serving as the bridge between customer intention and completed sale. Therefore, understanding various options and learning how to prioritize security can significantly enhance your online business's stability and credibility. In this chapter, we'll irrefutably dive deep into this multifaceted topic, taking care to lay bare the intricate details generally shrouded in tech-speak, for your complete understanding.

6.1. Overview of Online Payment Options

Online payment systems can be grouped into several categories based on their functionality. First off, we have traditional debit and credit card payments. These are usually processed via a payment gateway - a service that approves the card transaction. Payment gateboxes communicate between your website and your merchant account at a bank, ensuring that the customer's payment information is correct and that the funds are available.

Direct bank transfers also play a pivotal role in e-commerce, providing an option for those who prefer not to use credit or debit cards online. As the name suggests, payment is made directly from the customer's bank account to yours. Direct bank transfers are popular in many European countries, but the method varies from one geographical location to another.

E-wallets have emerged as another convenient payment option

widely used across e-commerce platforms. Services such as Paypal, Apple Pay, and Google Wallet fall into this category. Customers add their debit or credit card information to these digital wallets and can then pay for goods or services without having to enter their card details on various sites.

Cryptocurrency payments, although not as widespread, are also gradually gaining traction in the e-commerce world. Bitcoin and Ethereum are familiar names in this sector, offering a decentralized and potentially more secure method of payment.

6.2. Ensuring Secure Transactions

Maintaining a safe and secure transaction environment is paramount in establishing trust and encouraging repeat business. There exist various protocols and certifications aimed at ensuring not only the security of the transactions but also to provide assurance to the users that their data is safe.

Firstly, you should consider utilizing HTTPS (Hyper Text Transfer Protocol Secure) in your website. This is an encrypted version of HTTP, designed to protect the confidentiality and integrity of data between the user's computer and the site. The SSL certificate, which facilitates the HTTPS, ensures the sensitive information of your customers, such as credit card information, can't be intercepted by hackers.

Another mechanism in place is PCI DSS (Payment Card Industry Data Security Standard), a set of security standards designed to ensure all companies that accept, process, store or transmit credit card information, do so in a secure environment. This goes a long way in bolstering confidence in customers, knowing their transactions are protected.

3D Secure technology represents another level of security, adding an authentication step for online payments. Services like Visa's "Verified by Visa" and Mastercard's "SecureCode" offer this form of protection, ensuring the person making the transaction is the rightful card owner.

6.3. Challenges and Solutions in Online Payments

Like any system, online payments are not immune to challenges. Fraud is a pervasive issue in the e-commerce world, with criminals continually developing sophisticated methods to trick customers or steal data. A comprehensive fraud detection system is necessary to filter fraudulent transactions and reduce instances of chargebacks and disputes. Several AI-powered fraud detection solutions are available today, designed to enhance e-commerce fraud management.

Cross-border transactions introduce another set of challenges. Exchange rates and foreign transaction fees could negatively impact sales if not adequately managed or communicated. An effective solution is to have a multi-currency option, allowing customers to view and pay for products in their local currency, ensuring transparency and enhancing customer experience.

Technical glitches also represent a focal challenge. Down-times, slow loading times, or complicated checkout processes can lead customers to abandon their shopping carts. Therefore, e-stores should prioritize having seamless, straightforward, and quick checkout processes, facilitated by reliable hosting and consistent website maintenance.

With a thorough knowledge of online payment options, an understanding of security measures, and adaptability to overcome inherent challenges, successful online trading is within your grasp. To end with, remember: the customer's convenience and peace of mind should always be at the forefront, for, in e-commerce, customer satisfaction is paramount.

Chapter 7. Diving into Digital Marketing and SEO

Welcome to the magnificent world of digital marketing and SEO. In this deep dive, we will delve into the gamut of digital marketing strategies, explore the intricacies of search engine optimization (SEO), and discuss their importance in amplifying your online store's prominence. This chapter aims not just to enlighten you about the underlying concepts of digital marketing and SEO, but also to provide you with actionable steps to employ these strongholds in your e-commerce endeavors.

7.1. The Intricacies of Digital Marketing

Digital marketing refers to the utilization of online-based digital technologies and media for the promotion of products and services. In essence, it harnesses the power of the internet to connect with customers, thereby boosting conversions and fostering customer relationships. It envelops numerous strategies including content marketing, email marketing, social media marketing, pay-per-click (PPC), and more.

Content Marketing: Content marketing pivots on the creation and distribution of valuable, relevant, and consistent content to draw and retain a clearly defined audience, ultimately leading to profitable customer action. Content can take numerous formats, be it blog posts, how-to guides, infographics, videos, or podcasts.

Email Marketing: This strategy involves sending direct marketing messages via email to potential and current customers. It is an impactful way to foster relationships, promote brand loyalty, and amplify conversions.

Social Media Marketing: Social media platforms such as Facebook, Instagram, Pinterest, and LinkedIn, can be leveraged to promote products, interact with customers, and bolster your brand's online presence.

Pay-Per-Click (PPC): PPC is an online advertising model where advertisers pay for each click on their ads. This model can drive immediate results and traffic to your online store.

7.2. The Power of Search Engine Optimization (SEO)

SEO is the practice of refining your website's design and content to make it more attractive to search engines. The goal of SEO is for search engines to display your website as a top result on the search engine results page (SERP). There are several facets to SEO, including keyword optimization, quality content, and backlinks.

Keyword Optimization: Keywords refer to the phrases and words people use to search for products or services on search engines. By optimizing your website content and product descriptions with the correct keywords, you increase chances of your e-commerce store appearing in the search results.

Quality Content: High-quality, relevant content is favored by search engines and encourages visitors to stay on your site longer, which can improve your SEO ranking. This could include blog posts, how-to guides, product reviews, and more.

Backlinks: Backlinks play a significant role in SEO. They are links from other websites to yours, and they act like votes of confidence, signaling to search engines that your content is valuable.

7.3. Piecing It All Together: Digital Marketing and SEO in Action

Implementing digital marketing strategies in tandem with SEO can create high-reaching results. SEO forms the foundation of online visibility, while digital marketing uses this visibility to establish meaningful customer interactions and drive conversions.

For instance, carefully curated content boosted by a thorough keyword strategy can attract visitors to your site and improve SEO rankings. Supplementing this with regular email marketing campaigns can nurture relationships with these visitors, convince them of your products' value, and convert them into customers.

Likewise, utilizing PPC advertisements containing your SEO keywords can generate quick, immediate visibility and traffic for your store. Following up this visibility with interactive social media posts and updates can strengthen your brand's image among the customers and foster long-term relations.

In conclusion, the digital marketing landscape and SEO are vast domains with myriad components. Each part, when understood and utilized effectively, can fortify the popularity of your online store and galvanize e-commerce success. Armed with this comprehensive understanding of digital marketing and SEO, you are now equipped to dive into the bustling panorama of e-commerce and make your mark.

Chapter 8. Customer Engagement: Building Relationships That Last

Mastering the art of customer engagement isn't just about making a sale - it's about creating meaningful, lasting relationships with your customers that are steeped in trust, rapport, and consistency. Furnishing you with a deep-dive journey, this chapter ladles out the many facets of customer engagement, elucidating how each small connection stokes the embers of a sustaining relationship, urging your shoppers to return - again and again.

8.1. The Essentials of Customer Engagement

Customer engagement, much like a waltz, requires keen vision, an ear tuned to subtle cues, and a sequence inevitably leading towards a delightful end. To really grasp how to engage customers, you need to understand what it means to truly "engage". It means to hold attention, to captivate, to form bonds, to inform, and to inspire action, not intermittent but continuous.

The essence of customer engagement lies within three core principles: communication, personalization, and value creation. Let's pour over each one:

1. **Communication**: Keep your customers informed, show them that you're listening, and prove that their opinions matter.

2. **Personalization**: Tailor your interactions to meet individual customer needs and preferences, making each one feel valued and appreciated.

3. **Value Creation**: Provide more than just a product or service. Create experiences and offer resolutions that enhance overall customer satisfaction and brand loyalty.

8.2. Strategies for Effective Customer Engagement

Efficient customer engagement melds both the traditional and contemporary approaches to yield impactful and lasting relationships with your audience. Here are a few tactics you might find handy:

Using Social Media to Your Advantage: No longer just a millennial pastime, social media has emerged as a powerful platform for customer engagement. Forge connectivity, elicit feedback, broadcast announcements, and foster a sense of community.

Email Newsletters: Beyond pushing sales, newsletters have transformed into valuable educational resources, granting not just awareness about products but also narrating your brand's story and actualizing its personality.

Loyalty Programs: Reap commitment and earn repeat business by rewarding continued patronage. These programs can evoke a sense of exclusivity and instill a sentiment of belonging amongst customers.

Webinars and Live Q&As: Elaborating on products, answering queries in a real-time format, and educating customers can boost satisfaction and fuel engagement. It also fosters a sense of immediacy and rapport as customers feel directly connected to the brand.

8.3. Measuring Customer Engagement

Beyond strategies, it's critical to measure the effectiveness of your engagement efforts. Here are a few key metrics to consider:

Customer Satisfaction Score (CSAT): A survey metric that measures how happy customers are with your products or services.

Net Promoter Score (NPS): This index gauges customer willingness to recommend your brand to others, offering an understanding of customer loyalty.

Customer Churn Rate: This key performance indicator shows the percentage of customers who decided to stop using your service over a certain period.

Customer Retention Rate: This metric reveals the percentage of customers who have remained faithful to your brand over a specific period.

8.4. The Confluence of Customer Service and Engagement

An unmatched customer service strategy is the icing on your customer engagement cake. Here, the crux lies in resolution-driven interaction, swift response times, multiple touchpoints for customer contact, and a gentle nod towards customer feedback for improvement.

The concept of omnichannel customer service is gaining momentum. With customers reaching out on various platforms, the approach here is to offer a seamless, integrated, and consistent customer service experience across all channels–social media, email, phone or live chat. This not only enhances the customer interaction experience but also helps to build a stronger relationship.

8.5. Leveraging Technology for Customer Engagement

In the multifaceted world of e-commerce, your hand might feel forced to multitask, juggling several balls in the air. Fear not! Numerous technological tools can help alleviate the operational load while also enhancing customer engagement.

Artificial Intelligence (AI) and Chatbots: These can provide instant customer service–answering queries, resolving concerns, and even upselling–all the while collecting invaluable data which can then be analyzed to improve services further.

Customer Relationship Management (CRM) Software: Provides a centralized platform that organizes customer interactions, enabling personalized service and fostering crucial insights on customer behavior.

8.6. The Road Ahead: The Future of Customer Engagement

The future of customer engagement seems pointed towards an even more personalized and integrated experience. Technological advances are tipping more towards AI bots and Virtual Reality for offering immersive customer experiences. Intertwining it with measures that boost ethics and sustainability might just be the next big thing. Data analytics and predictive modeling will play a crucial part in shaping a deeply targeted engagement approach.

Finding your way treading through the labyrinth of customer relationships may seem complex, but with clear direction, empathy-driven interaction, and the right tools, you would soon find yourself navigating with ease, creating lasting, impressionable connections.

Remember, good customer engagement is like a well-told story, one that charms, enchants, and invites you back for more. Being the protagonist of this narrative, the onus lies on you, not to just sell, but to also captivate and retain customers, thereby writing a story that's unique to every customer, each narrating their unique tale.

Chapter 9. Shipping and Logistics: Overcoming Cross Border Challenges

The rise of e-ccmmerce has ushered in an era of borderless shopping. However, cross-border commercial transactions do come with their own set of challenges. Shipping and logistics inevitably take center stage when overcoming these hurdles, bearing the weight of the customer's final touchpoint with your brand.

9.1. Understanding Cross-border Shipping

Cross-border shipping refers to the process of transporting goods from a seller in one country to a buyer in another. This process involves multiple stages, each with its own complexities, including the exporting and importing of goods, customs clearance, local delivery, and returns management.

A robust cross-border shipping strategy is critical to maintaining customer satisfaction and loyalty. The intricacies of shipping dynamics such as cost, security, time efficiency, and tracking can significantly impact the overall customer experience.

9.2. Factoring In Shipping Costs

The cost of shipping products cross-border can be a significant portion of the total expense involved in an e-commerce transaction. It's vital to consider various costs such as packaging, freight, insurance, duties, taxes, and handling fees. Merchants must strike a balance between absorbing these costs and passing them along to the customers, aiming to maintain profitability while avoiding sky-high prices that repel customers.

Consider offering free shipping for orders over a certain value, or integrating real-time shipping calculators into your e-commerce platform. These calculators factor in variables such as package dimensions, weight, destination, and desired delivery speed, providing customers with transparency around shipping costs.

9.3. Navigating Customs and Duties

When shipping internationally, understanding customs regulations, import duties, and taxes is crucial. These elements may vary significantly between countries and can substantially change the total cost of the shipped product. An informed seller could utilize Delivered Duty Paid (DDP) or Delivered Duty Unpaid (DDU) models in order to create a smoother transaction process for the customer.

DDP means the seller assumes all responsibility and costs for delivering goods to buyers and pays all import customs charges before shipping. The advantage is that customers receive their products without any extra unexpected expenses, enhancing customer satisfaction. However, DDP can be more complex for the seller because they will have to handle customs paperwork and deal with any potential issues related to import regulations.

On the other hand, DDU means the buyer is liable for the customs charges on arrival. While this model removes the seller's obligations concerning customs, it might create a potentially unpleasant surprise for the customer upon product arrival. Transparency and clear communication of which model your business employs will contribute to a positive customer experience.

9.4. Managing Transit Times

Transit time—the period from when a product leaves the warehouse to when it arrives at the buyer's doorstep—is another critical factor. Managing expectations around delivery schedules is key to retaining your customers' trust. Offering various shipping options—from slower, budget-friendly choices to faster, more expensive ones—is an effective way to meet different customer needs and preferences.

9.5. Tracking and Transparency

In today's e-commerce world, customers expect to be kept informed about their order's status. It's not just about providing a tracking number anymore; many customers appreciate frequent and proactive updates. Notify them at every major milestone: order confirmation, dispatch, transit, delivery, and follow-up. A satisfied customer is the best advert for your business

9.6. Returns and Refunds

Returns are inevitable in the world of e-commerce. Making the returns process seamless and simple for cross-border purchases can be a challenge but is a must if customer satisfaction and retention are your goals. One solution could be working with international returns facilitators or using local collection points in the customer's country. Ensure to clearly articulate your returns policy, including timelines, condition requirements, and whether the buyer or seller will bear the return shipping costs on your website.

9.7. Leveraging Technology

The use of technology in shipping and logistics can simplify cross-border transactions. Tools for tracking, handling documentation, calculating taxes and duties, and managing returns can streamline the process and provide data that helps refine your strategy. Exploring and investing in technology solutions tailored to your business needs could create a smoother, more efficient shipping experience for both you and your customers.

9.8. Preparing for Challenges

Regardless of a well-structured cross-border shipping strategy, unexpected challenges can arise. These could range from delays due to weather or holidays, lost or damaged parcels, discrepancies in order tracking, and changes in customs regulations. Anticipating such issues, having contingency plans, and being proactive in communicating with customers is key to navigating them effectively.

In conclusion, while cross-border shipping and logistics can present significant challenges, they also provide unique opportunities to expand market reach, diversify the customer base, and increase profitability. Through careful planning, strategic decision-making, and excellent customer communication, e-commerce businesses can master these complexities and thrive on a global scale.

Chapter 10. Deciphering Analytics: The Heartbeat of Your E-commerce Store

In the pulsating world of e-commerce, analytics serves as the lifeblood that powers your online store, painting a vivid picture of customer behaviour, product performance, and much more. Deciphering this intricate web of information may seem like a daunting task, but fear not! With the right understanding and tools at your disposal, you can tune into the heartbeat of your store and use these insights to fuel your success.

10.1. Getting Started with E-commerce Analytics

E-commerce analytics involves the collection, analysis, and presentation of data from your online store. This data relates to buying behaviour, customer interaction, expenditure, and other key indicators that provide a comprehensive snapshot of your store's performance. To begin, familiarize yourself with your platform's built-in analytics dashboard. Here, you'll encounter numerous metrics, each contributing a distinct piece to your store's story.

10.2. Metrics That Matter

There are countless data points to track, but some resonate louder than others. Lady e-commerce entrepreneur, your focus should gravitate towards these crucial metrics:

1. **Traffic**: This relates to the number of visitors your online store receives. High traffic could point towards successful marketing

efforts or popular products, while a drop could be a red flag that needs immediate attention.

2. **Conversion Rate**: This is the percentage of visitors who complete a desired action — a sale, for instance. A low conversion rate amidst high traffic can indicate a disconnect somewhere in the customer journey.

3. **Average Order Value (AOV)**: This metric computes the average total of each completed order. A high AOV signals that customers are spending more on each purchase.

4. **Cart Abandonment Rate**: When customers add products to their online shopping cart but exit before completing the purchase, this leads to cart abandonment. A high abandonment rate could speak to a complicated checkout process or hidden costs.

5. **Customer Retention Rate**: This measures the number of customers who make repeat purchases from your store. A high retention rate can signify customer satisfaction and loyalty.

10.3. Simplicity Amid Complexity: Interpreting Data

Once you have your key stats, the real challenge becomes interpreting what they say about your business. This task requires context. For example, a high abandonment rate might seem discouraging. However, when paired with an unusually complicated checkout process, it becomes clear that it's an area needing improvement rather than a reflection of ineffective marketing.

To simplify this process, you can utilize data visualization tools such as graphs, heatmaps, or pie charts. These make patterns and trends more noticeable, and you can make data-driven decisions with greater confidence.

10.4. Implementing and Tracking Changes

After you interpret your data, it's time to implement changes. Remember, the goal is not to heap drastic modifications on your store, but to refine existing processes based on your newfound knowledge. Small, incremental changes oftentimes yield the most positive results.

Following changes, closely track your metrics to gauge their effect. Be patient and allow for enough time to glean accurate insights. Remember, analytics is an ongoing process, not a one-time event.

10.5. From Analytics to Action: Case Studies

Instances abound where e-commerce stores used analytics to monumental advantage.

For example, using analytics, an online clothes retailer noticed a high portion of their traffic was from mobile devices, but their conversion rate was significantly lower in this segment. They used this insight to overhaul their mobile interface, making it more user-friendly and driving up conversion rates among mobile shoppers.

This demonstrates the power of analytics: it identifies problem areas and equips you with the information to remedy them, catalyzing success in your e-commerce venture.

In conclusion, e-commerce analytics, when deciphered correctly, illuminates the path towards enhanced performance and profitability. It's a journey of discovery, full of fascinating revelations about your customers, your products, and ultimately, your business. Embrace this journey with open arms and watch as your e-commerce store transforms in line with the insights you glean. Analytics doesn't have to be intimidating – armed with the right knowledge and tools, it becomes a powerful conduit for business evolution.

Chapter 11. Facing the Future: Keeping Up with E-commerce Trends

In this dynamic e-commerce cosmos, adaptability is the key to surviving and thriving. What worked yesterday might not necessarily reap the same result today, which emphasizes the importance of being in tune with evolving technology, consumer behaviour, scoring trends, and market forecasts. This update doesn't mean dismissing everything you know so far, but rather, sprinkling your existing knowledge base with shiny new inputs. So fasten your seat belts as we embark on an insightful journey to uncover future trends in e-commerce!

11.1. Embracing Automation

In an age marked by technological advancements, automation is no longer a choice; it's a necessity. From customer service to inventory management, automation helps in reducing human errors and enhancing efficiency. More crucially, it frees up your time letting you focus on core areas that would benefit from your personal touch.

Chatbots, for instance, are gaining momentum in the online space. These digital assistants can handle a range of tasks, like answering customer queries in real-time, guiding them through their shopping journey, and even upselling and cross-selling products. Automation tools in inventory management and pricing can help reduce overstock and understock situations, ensuring a seamless supply-demand chain. Let's not forget about e-mail marketing automation, which helps businesses interact with their customers more efficiently and with a personal touch.

Therefore, embrace automation, welcome a hassle-free e-commerce existence, and keep up with rivals within the industry.

11.2. Customer-Centric Shopping Experience

A customer-centric shopping experience is the axis around which future e-commerce trends revolve. This includes personalised shopping experiences, improved product visuals, voice search, and mobile shopping.

With data analytics, we can access valuable customer information, which can aid in providing a more personalised shopping experience. It's a way of showing customers that you understand and appreciate them, which can, in turn, encourage their loyalty towards your online store.

Product visualization has also stepped up. Given the lack of physical interaction in e-commerce, working on product imagery, augmented reality and 3D visualizations can provide the customers with a comprehensive understanding of what they are buying, thereby creating a more satisfying shopping experience.

The advent of voice assistants like Siri, Alexa and Google Assistant has led to a rise in voice search. By optimizing your website for voice search, you ensure that your business doesn't miss out on access to this growing market segment.

11.3. Escalating Importance of Mobile Commerce

Today's consumers are constantly on-the-go, fostering an environment where mobile commerce is more popular than ever. It's projected to claim an increasing share of e-commerce sales, prompting businesses to design mobile responsive websites and apps.

But mobile commerce is not just about owning a mobile application; it involves providing a seamless shopping experience on the mobile platform. This may include features like mobile wallets for effortless payment and rewards programs that keep mobile users coming back for more.

11.4. Environmental Sustainability

With more customers becoming environmentally conscious, e-commerce businesses are expected to step up their game in this area. Green shipping, plastic-free packaging, fast fashion curbing are some of the measures to align your e-commerce store with sustainable practices.

Offering recycled or sustainable products can lure in eco-conscious buyers, and a 'green' digital marketing approach can genuinely enhance your business's reputation while also fostering better relationships with environmentally aware customers.

11.5. Big Data and Predictive Analytics

In the realm of e-commerce, data is the king. Using big data effectively can unveil customer behaviour patterns that can aid in creating effective marketing strategies. This could mean anything from the most visited pages on your site to the products most added to carts.

Predictive analytics use this big data, along with machine learning algorithms, to predict future trends and behaviours, thereby creating a tailored experience for shoppers and taking personalization to another dimension.

11.6. Blockchain Technology

Blockchain technology is another emerging trend that could revolutionize e-commerce – particularly in terms of payments and security. It offers the prospect of executing transparent, secure, and hassle-free transactions. With customer trust being integral to e-commerce, businesses that leverage blockchain might just have a competitive advantage.

In conclusion, keeping up with e-commerce trends ensures that you navigate this vibrant, complex world with ease and profitability. Remember, trends evolve to cater to the changing consumer behavior and preferences, thus ensuring you stay on top of them can be your key to consistently meet and exceed your customers' expectations, driving your e-commerce journey towards growth and success.

www.ingramcontent.com/pod-product-compliance
Lightning Source LLC
Chambersburg PA
CBHW070140230526
45472CB00004B/1615